EYE DEVELOPMENT

+

BRAIN DEVELOPMENT

+

EXTENDED TUMMY TIME

+

IMPROVED ATTENTION SPAN

+

ENHANCES TRACKING ABILITIES

=

HELLO BUGS

Hello

Ant

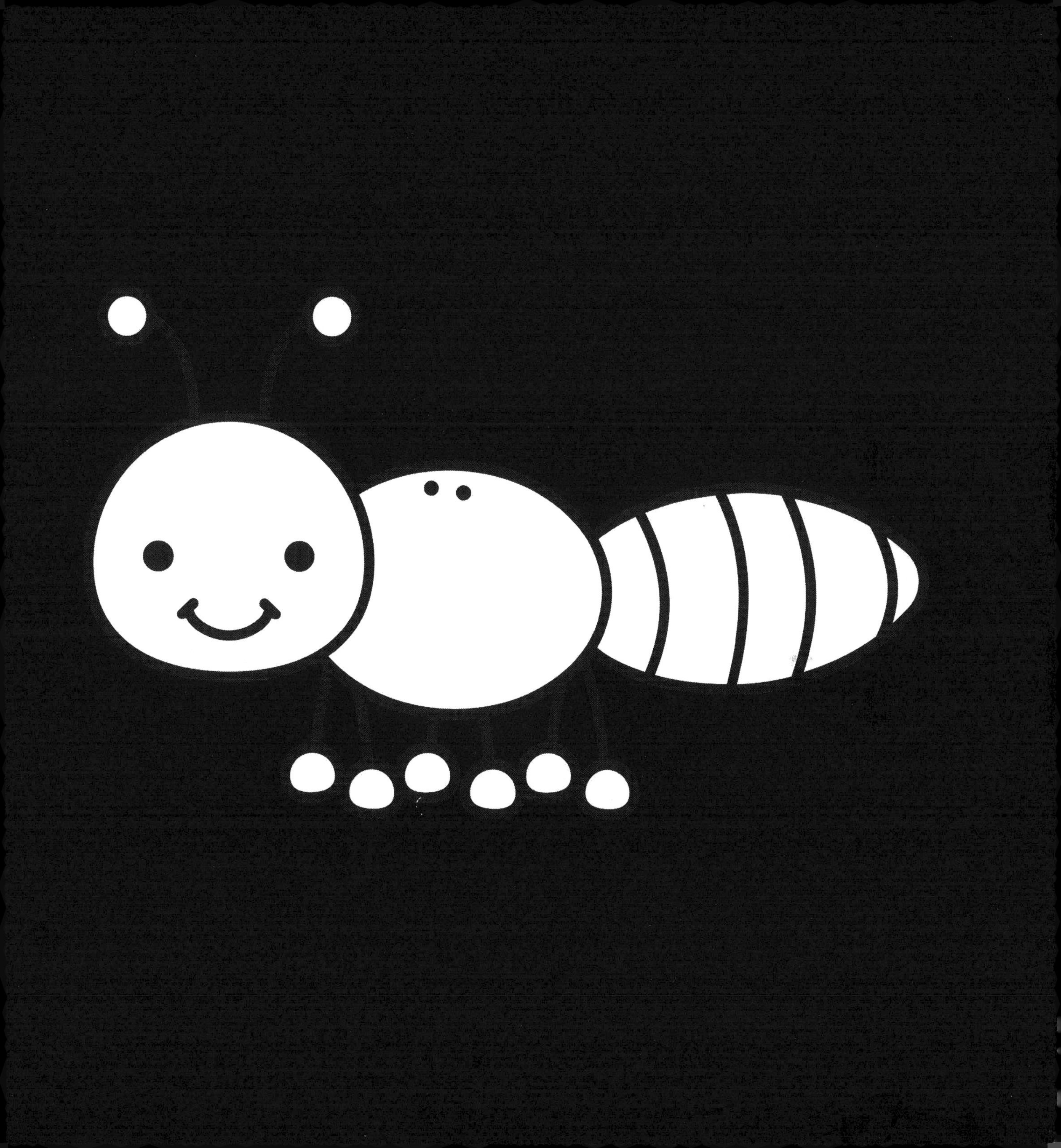

Hello

Bee

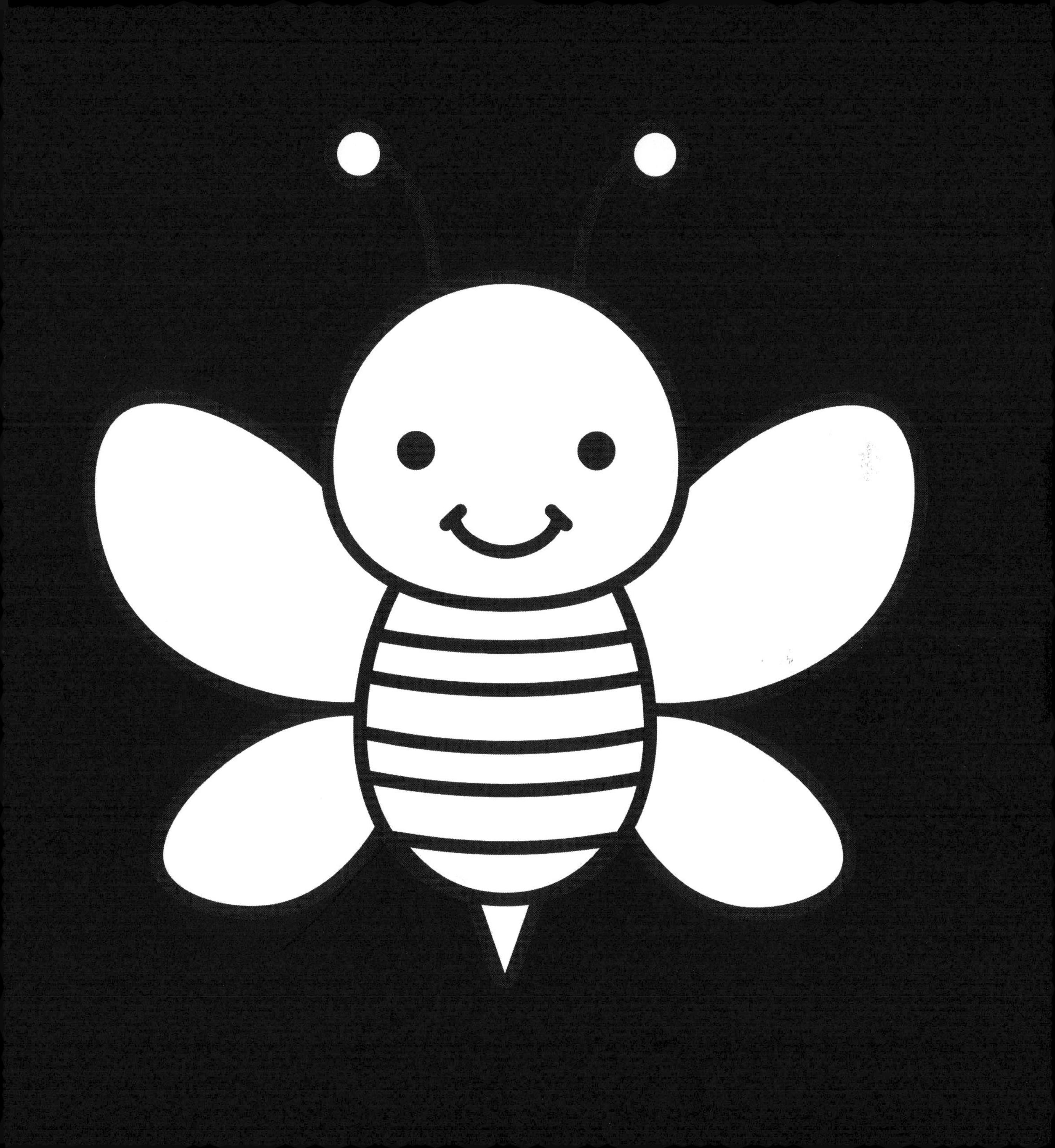

Hello

Butterfly

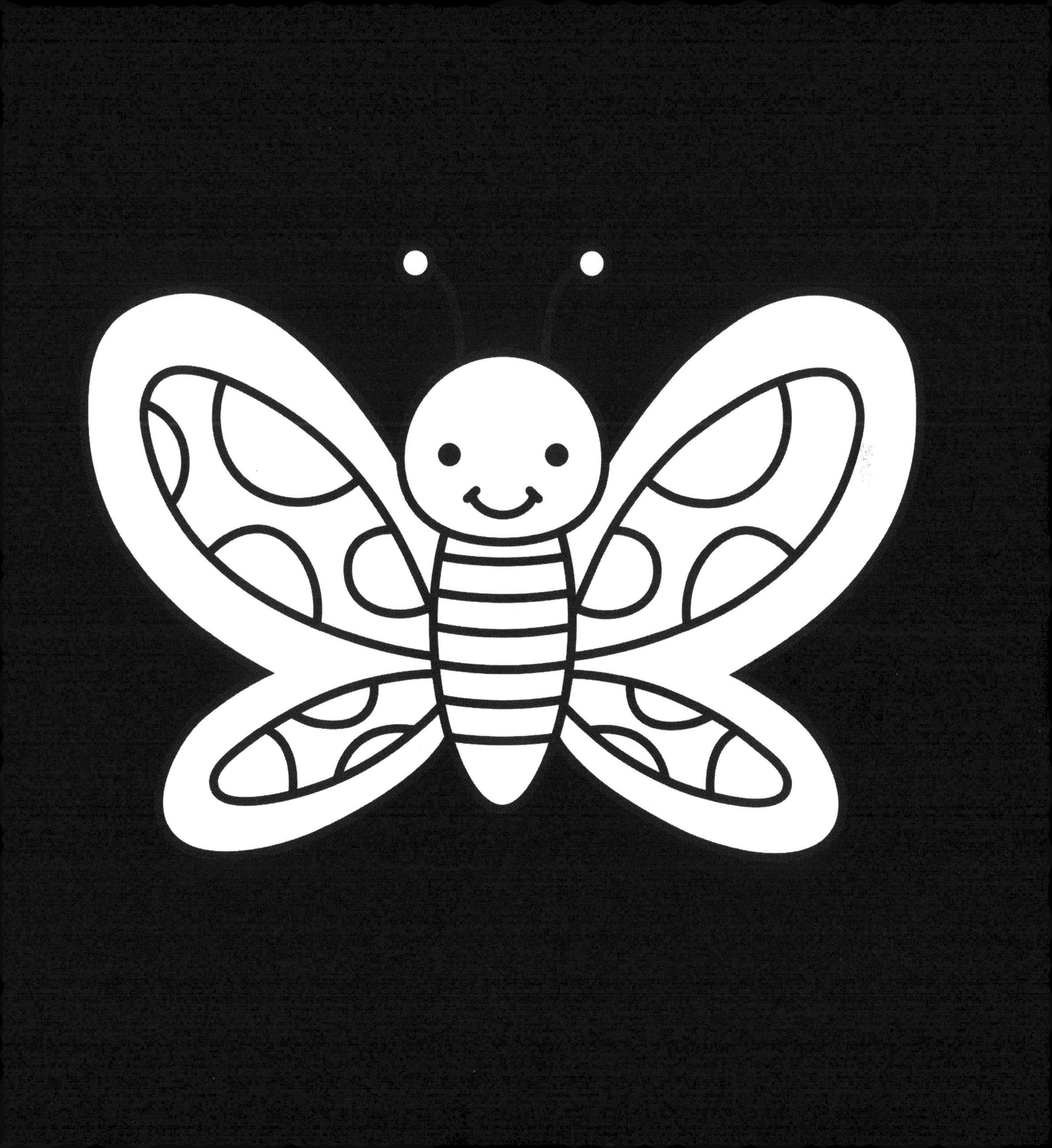

Hello

Beetle

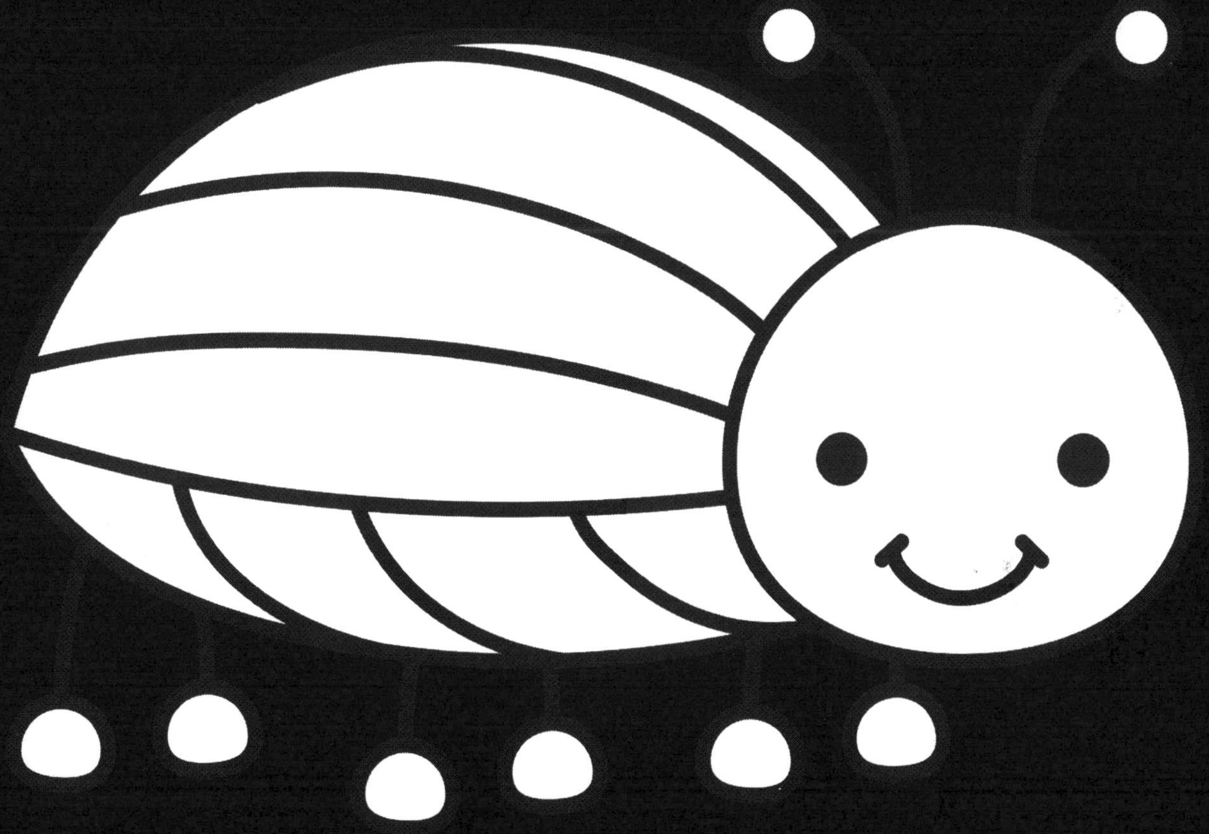

Hello

Caterpillar

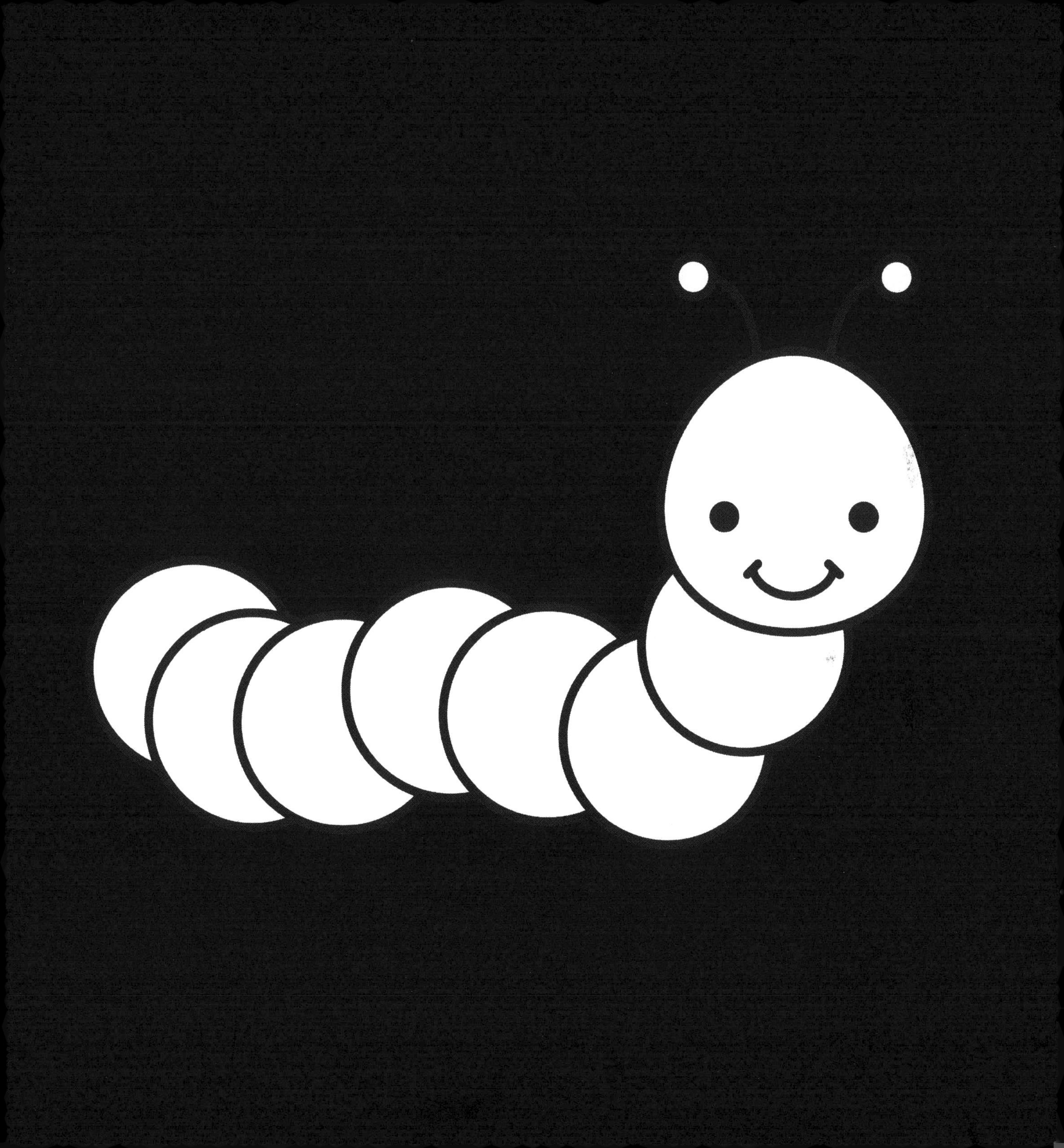

Hello

Cricket

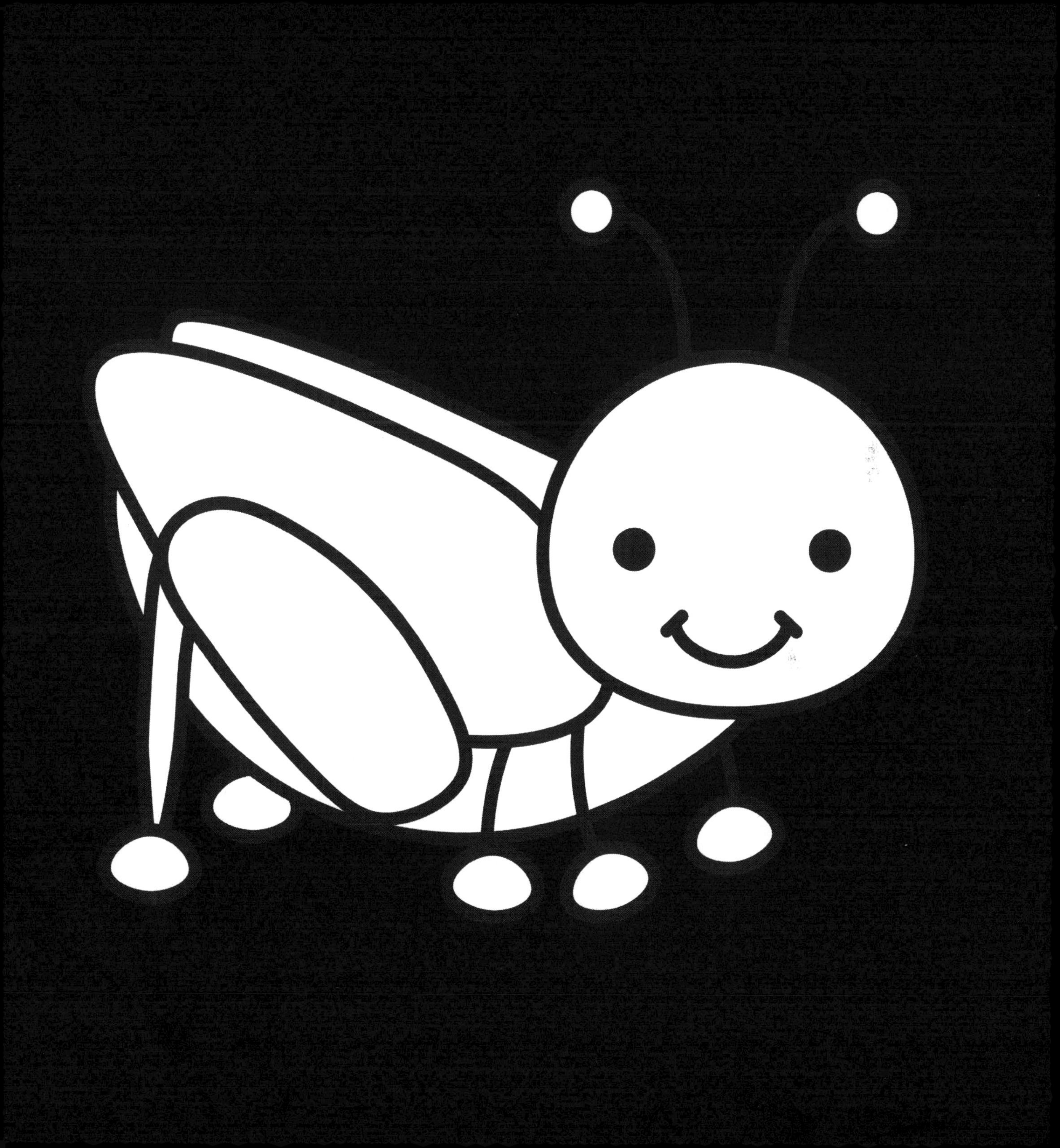

Hello

Fly

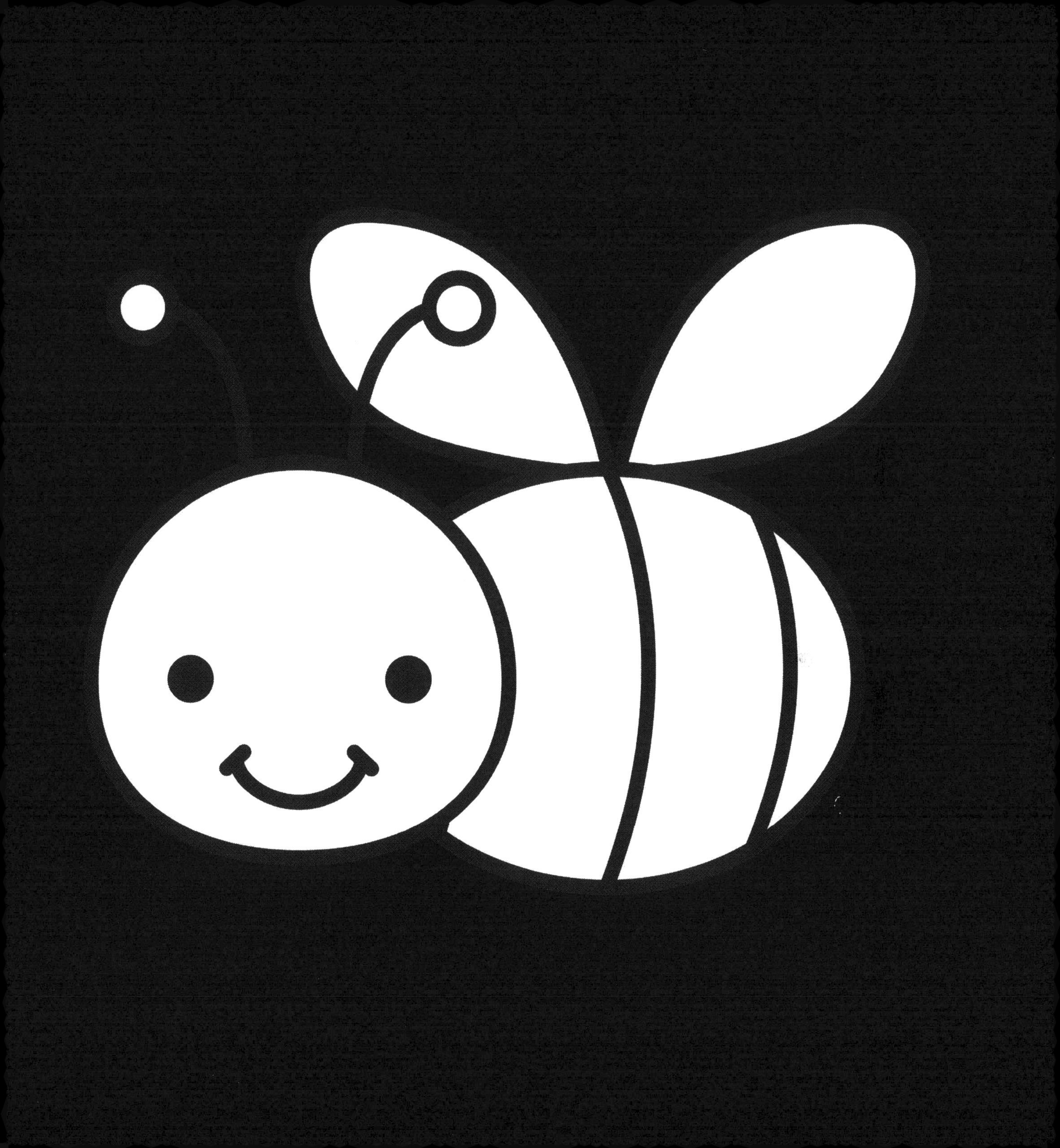

Hello

Ladybug

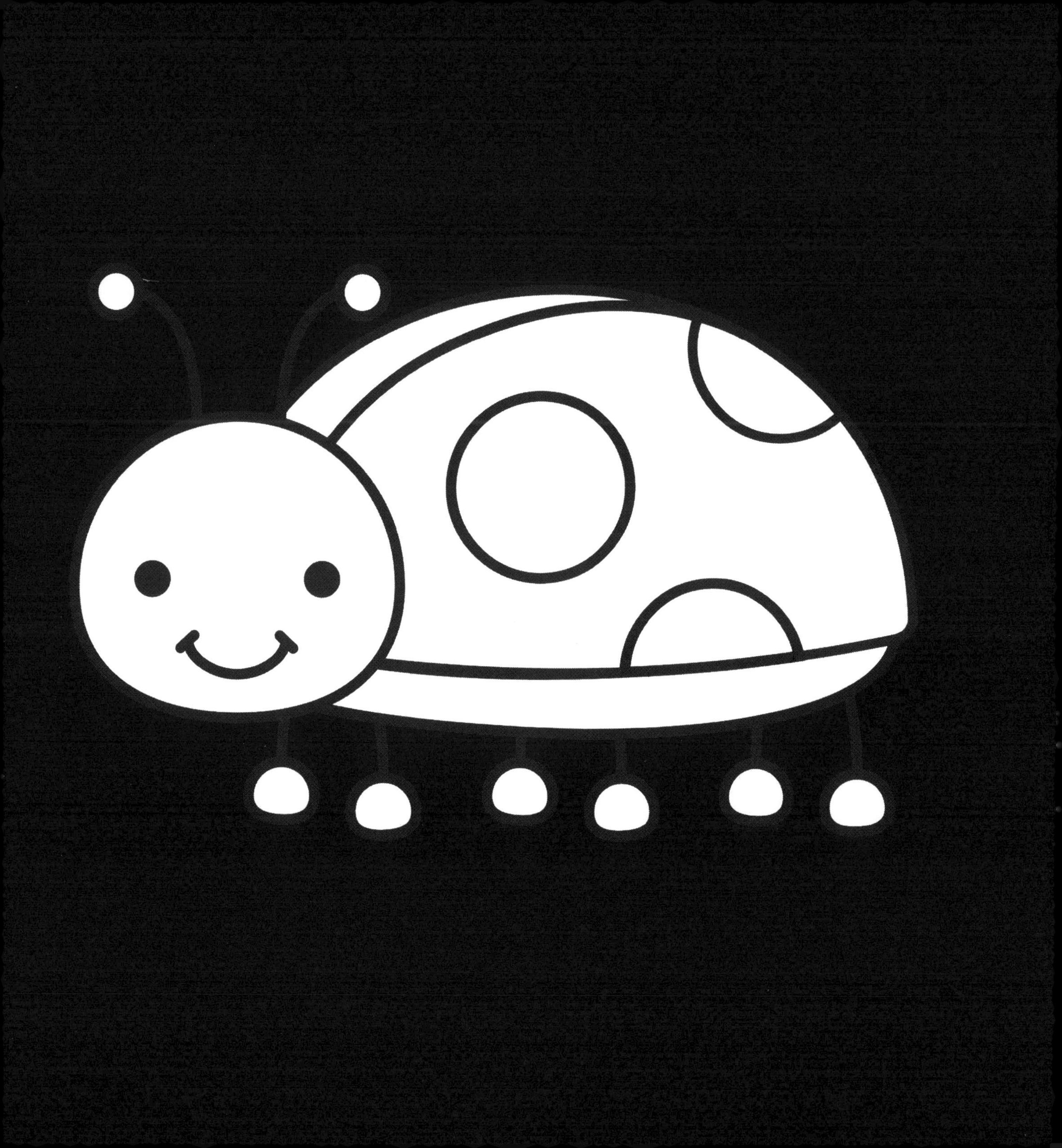

Hello

Grub

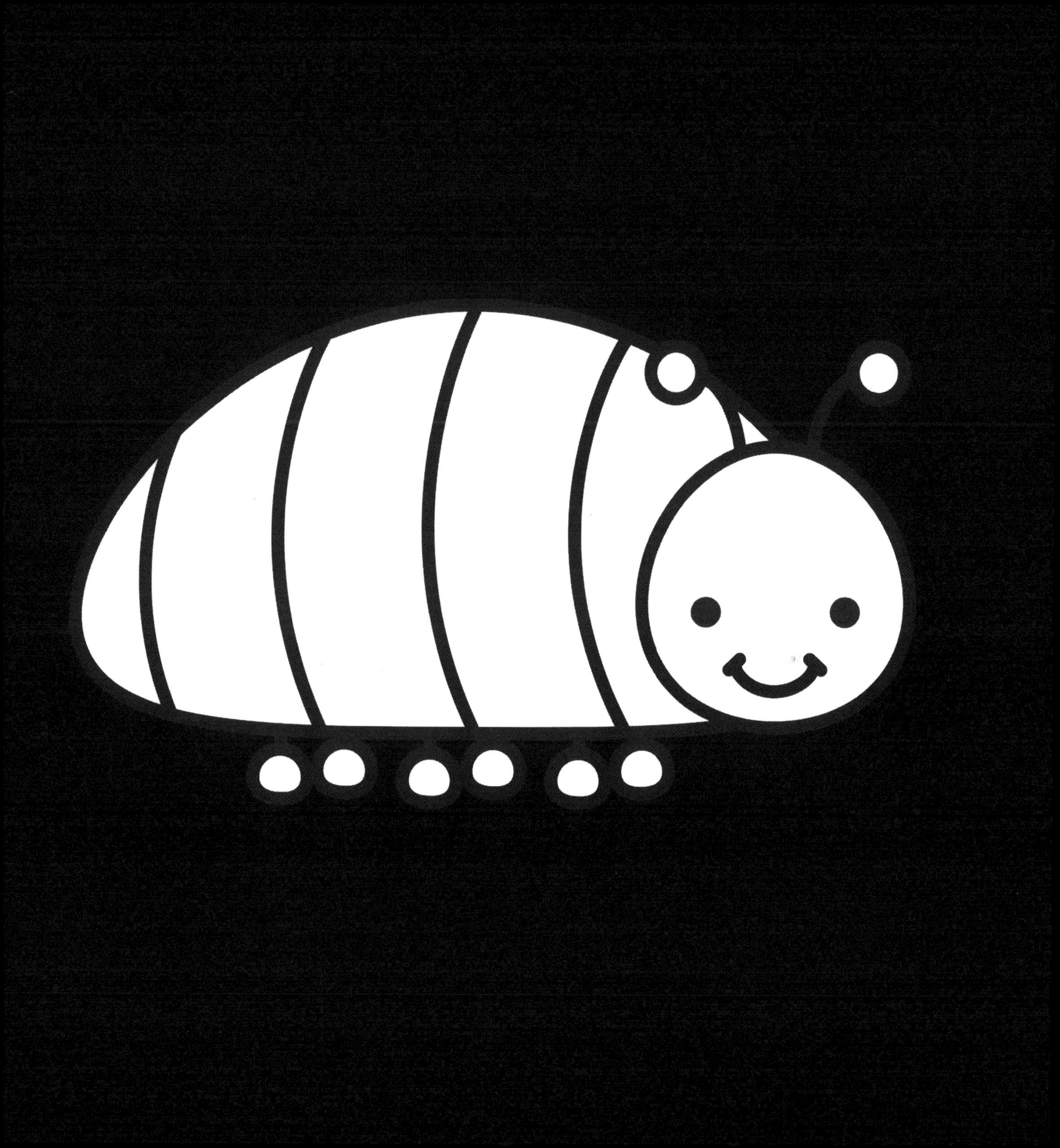

Hello

Snail

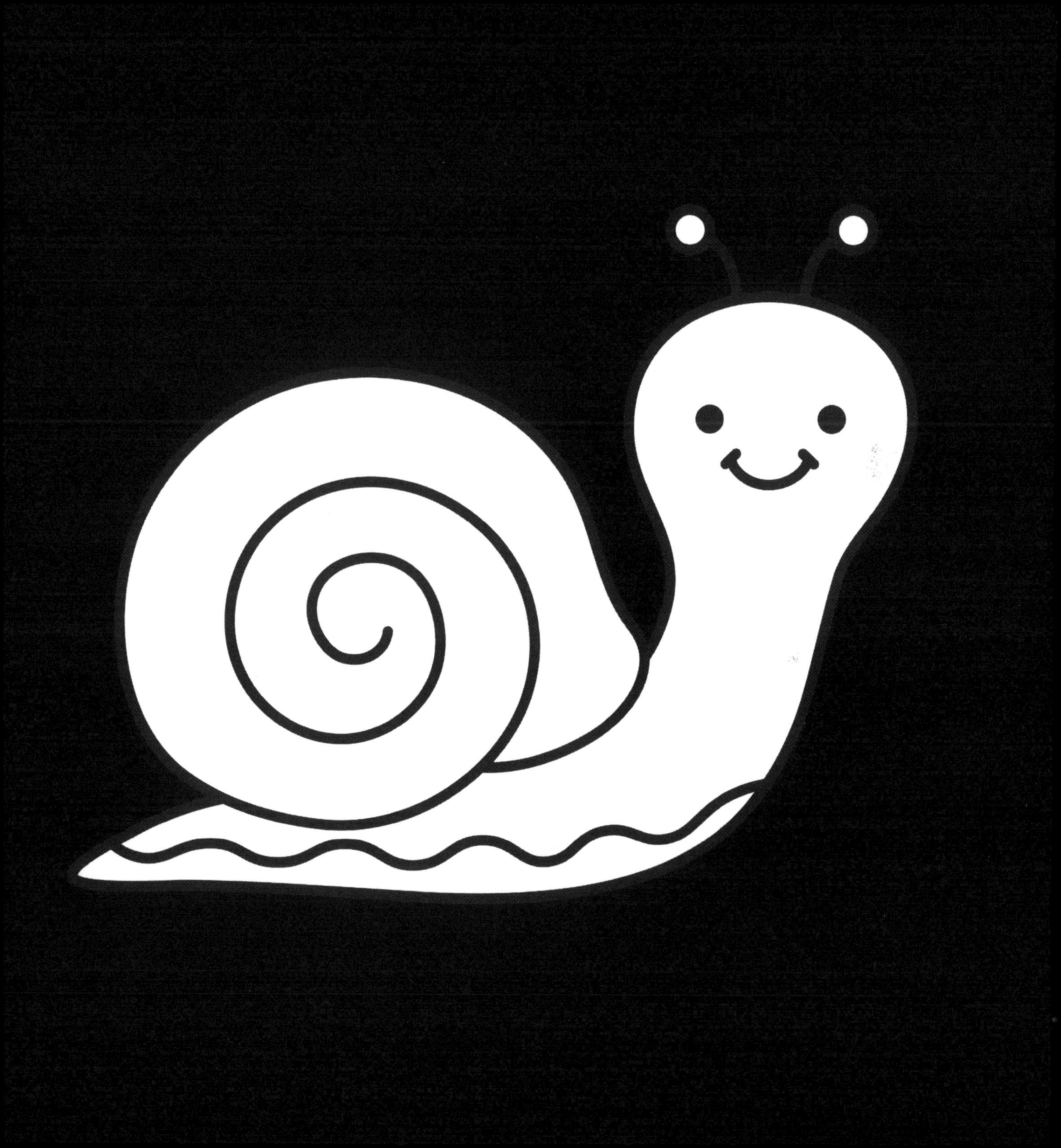

Hello

Spider

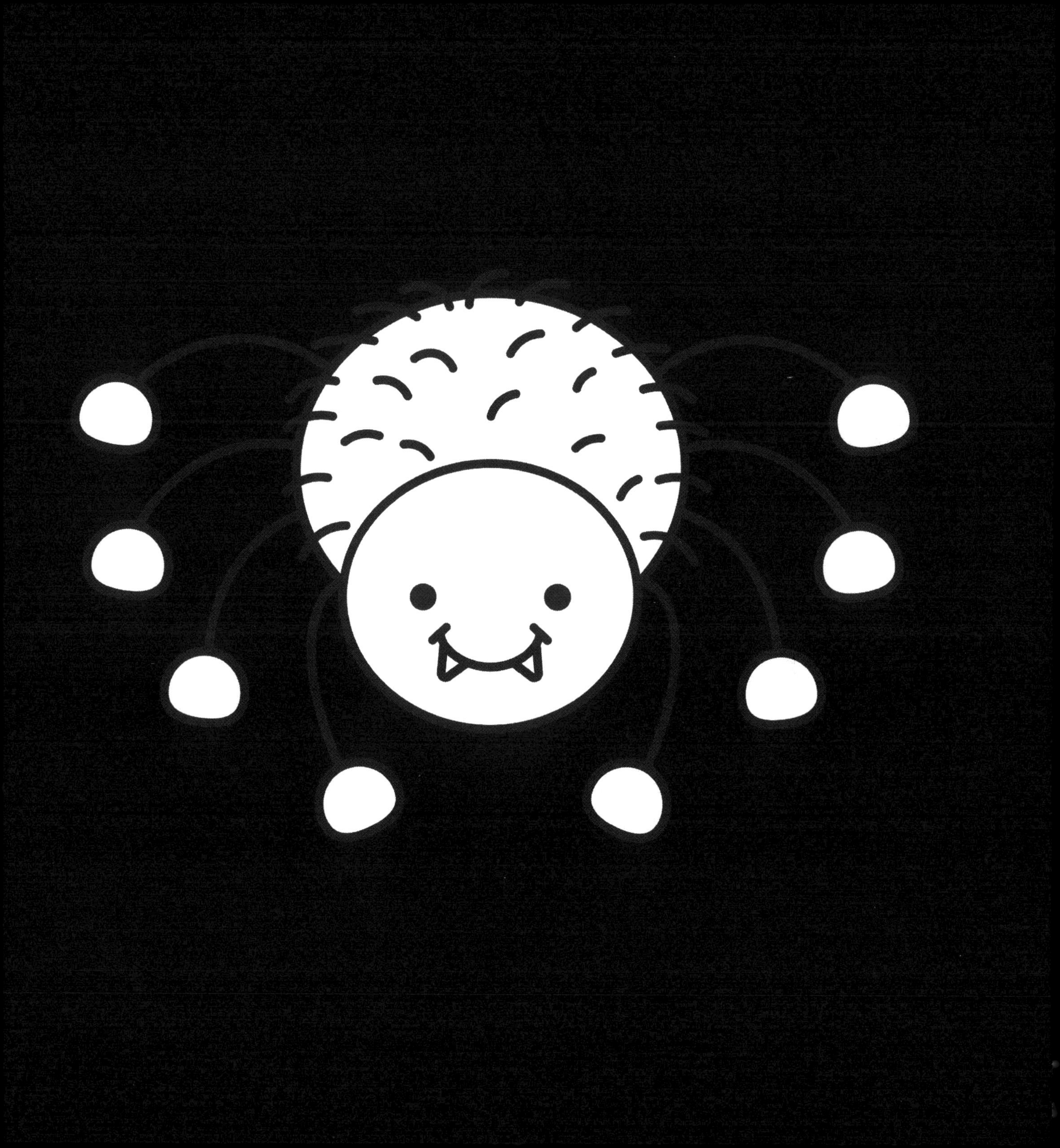

Hello

Worm

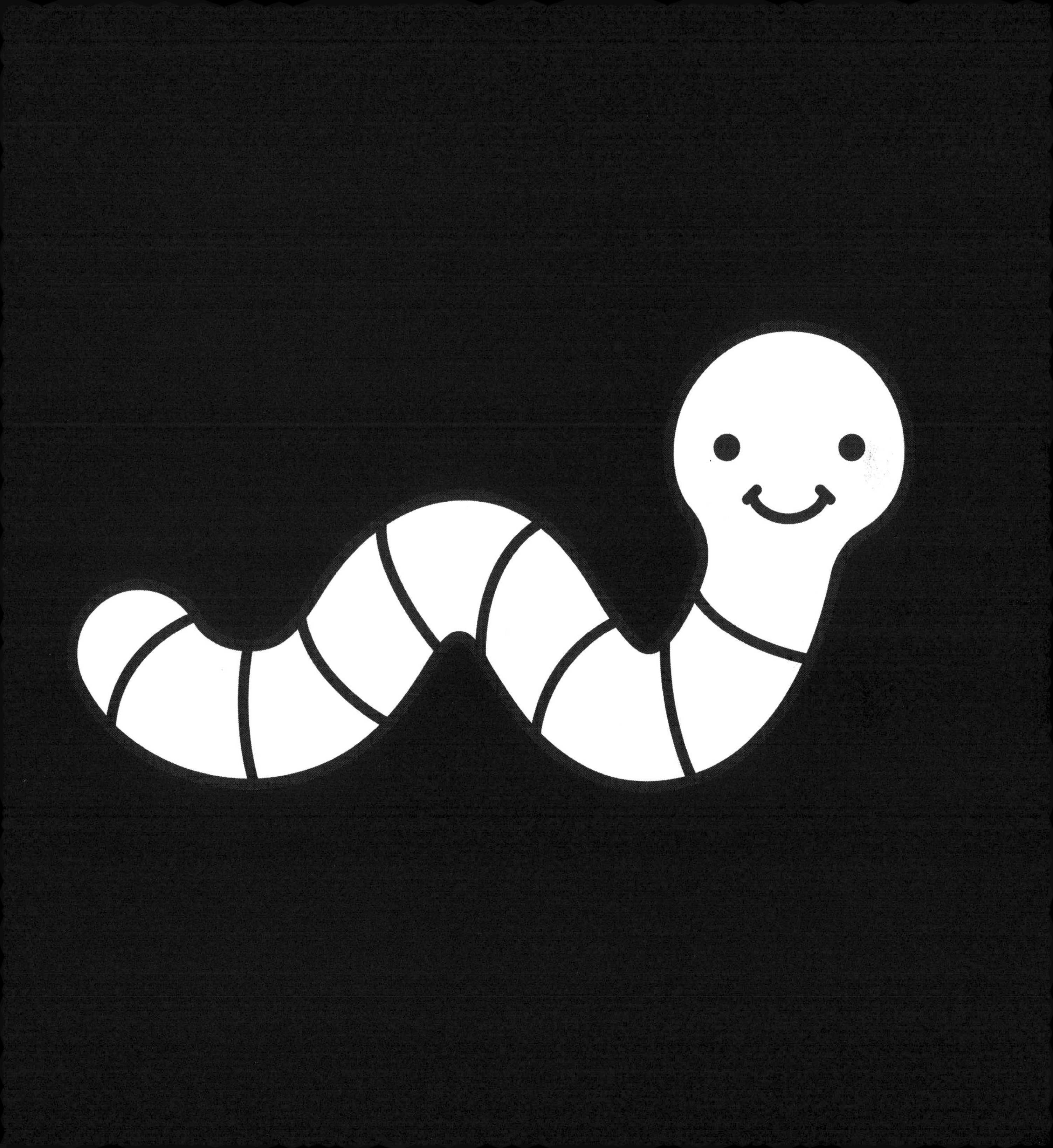

Hello

Slug

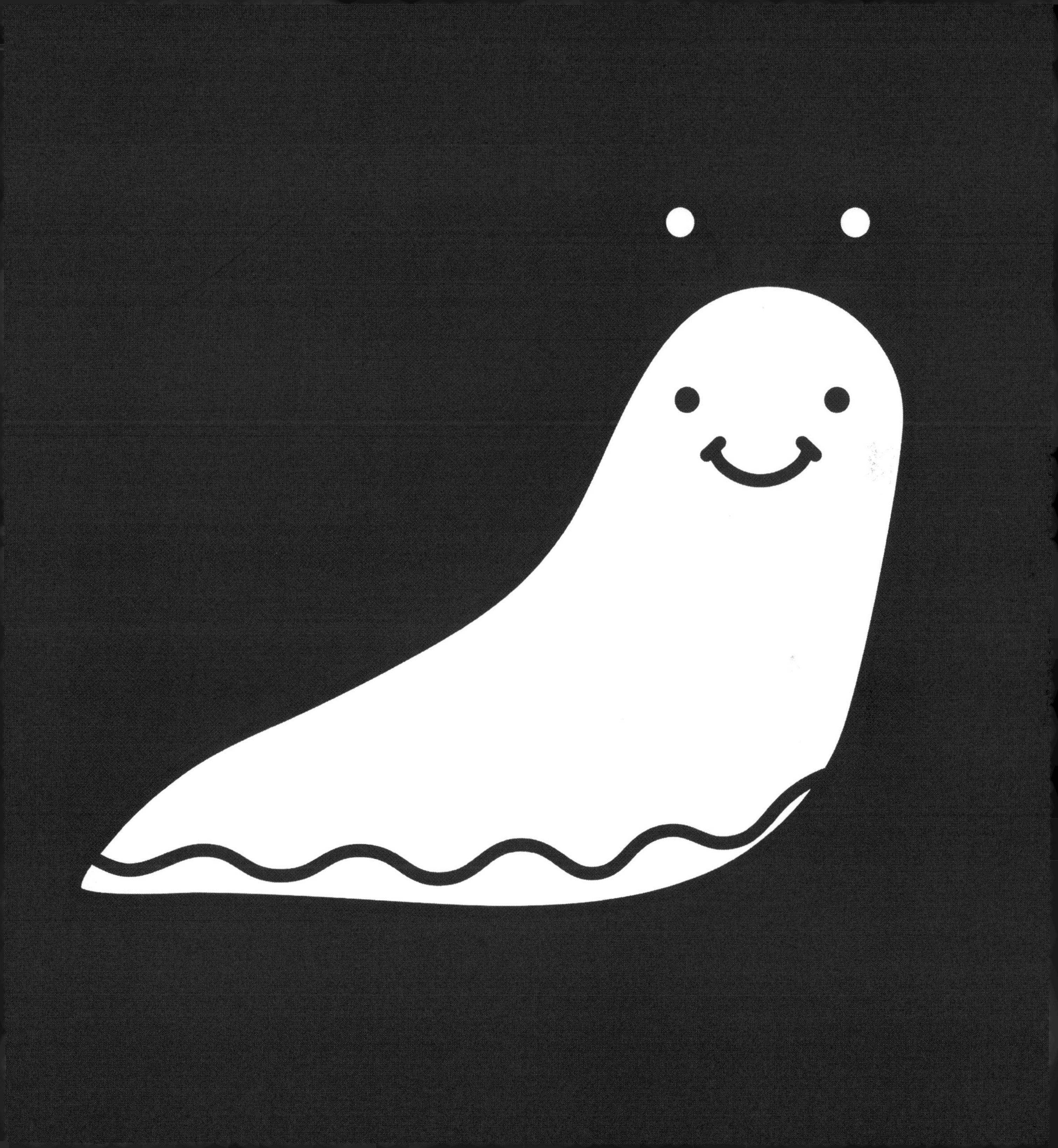

Hello

Dragonfly

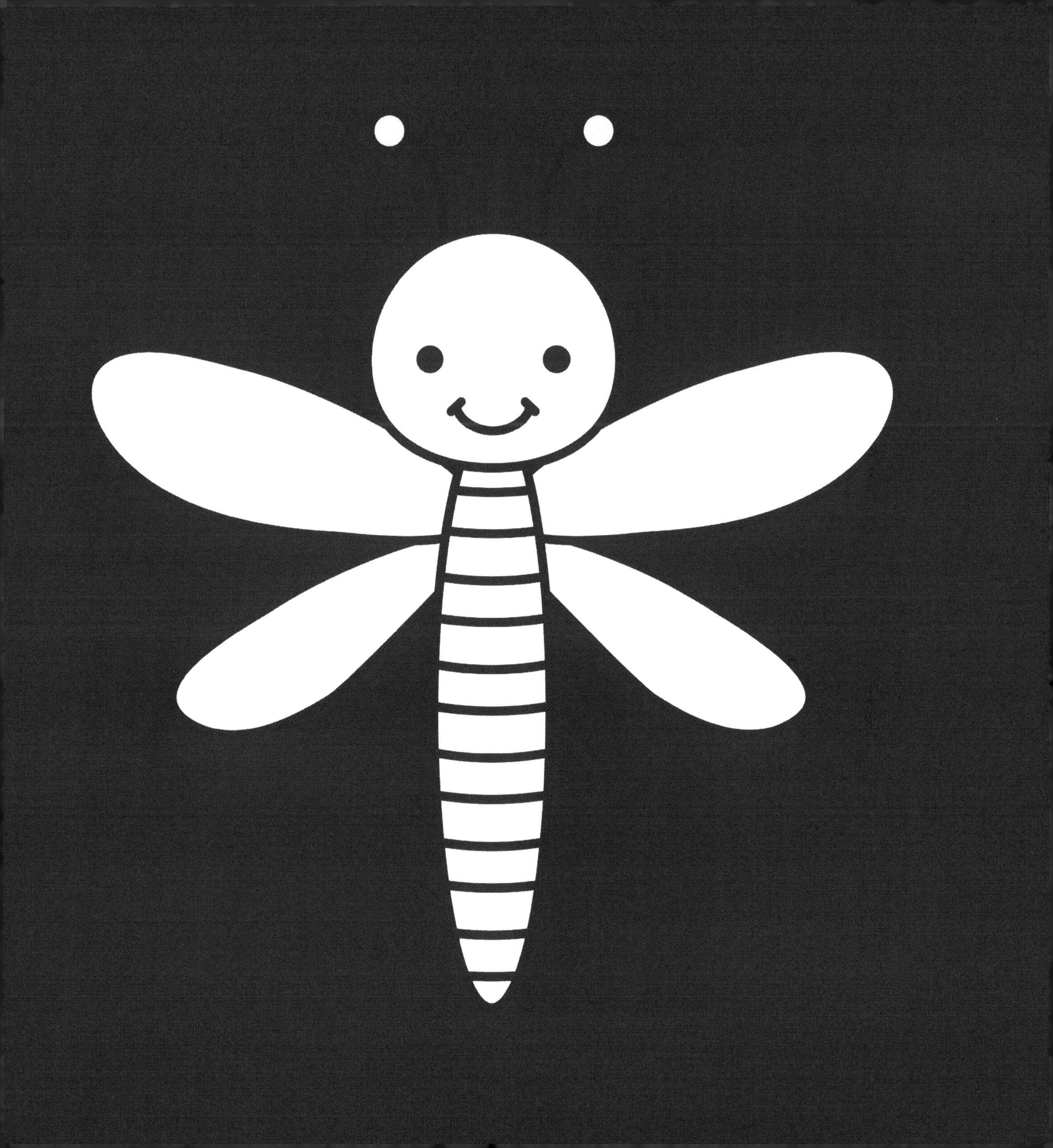

THANK YOU FOR GETTING OUR BOOK !

IF YOU FIND THIS BOOK FUN AND USEFUL, WE WOULD BE VERY GREATFUL IF YOU POSTED A SHORT REVIEW ON AMAZON :)

YOUR SUPPORT DOES MAKE A DIFFERENCE AND WE READ EVERY REVIEW PERSONALLY.

ALSO YOU CAN FIND US ON FACEBOOK.

THANK YOU FOR YOUR SUPPORT.

Magical Lake

Printed in Great Britain
by Amazon